THE EMPIRE
BATTLE OF MIDWAY
FALLS

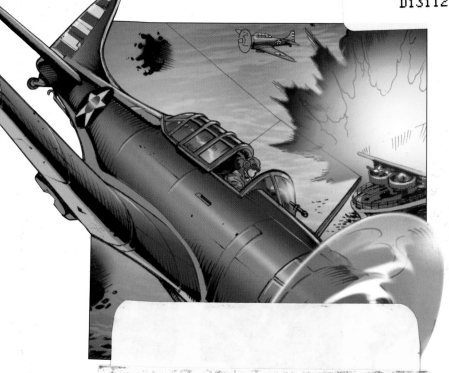

Richard Elson's Dedication

For Harvey. I think you would have enjoyed this one.

First published in Great Britain in 2006 by Osprey Publishing,
Midland House, West Way, Botley, Oxford OX2 0PH, UK
443 Park Avenue South, New York, NY 10016, USA
E-mail: info@ospreypublishing.com

A CIP catalog record for this book is available from the British Library

ISBN-10: 1 84603 058 7
ISBN-13: 978 1 84603 058 1

Page layout by Osprey Publishing
Map by The Map Studio
Originated by United Graphics Pte Ltd, Singapore
Printed in China through Bookbuilders

06 07 08 09 10   10 9 8 7 6 5 4 3 2 1

FOR A CATALOG OF ALL BOOKS PUBLISHED BY OSPREY PUBLISHING
PLEASE CONTACT:

NORTH AMERICA
Osprey Direct, c/o Random House Distribution Center, 400 Hahn Road,
Westminster, MD 21157, USA
E-mail: info@ospreydirect.com

ALL OTHER REGIONS
Osprey Direct UK, P.O. Box 140 Wellingborough, Northants, NN8 2FA, UK
E-mail: info@ospreydirect.co.uk

www.ospreypublishing.com

CONTENTS

WHO'S WHO

Admiral Isoroku Yamamoto (1884–1943) was commander of the Japanese Imperial Navy and mastermind behind the attack on Pearl Harbor and the invasion of Midway.

Admiral Chester Nimitz (1885–1966) was the U.S. Pacific Fleet's Commander in Chief, and he turned the U.S. Navy into a successful fighting machine after the Japanese attack on Pearl Harbor.

Vice-Admiral Chuichi Nagumo (1887–1944) was an admiral in the Imperial Japanese Navy and Commander of the First Air Fleet at Pearl Harbor and Midway. Following the defeat at Midway and later battles, he killed himself in 1944.

Rear Admiral Frank Fletcher (1885–1973) was overall commander of Task Force 16 and 17 carrier forces of the U.S. Pacific Fleet at Midway. Although victorious at Midway, superiors believed that he was too cautious, and was relieved of duty. He was assigned commander of the Northern Pacific Area.

WORLD WAR 2 1939-1945

The Japanese attack on the U.S. naval base at Pearl Harbor, Hawaii, in December 1941, dragged America into a war that had already been going on in Europe and Asia for two years. America was not fully prepared for battle, because it had tried to stay out of the war.

In the months immediately after Pearl Harbor, Japanese forces conquered many places in and around the Pacific such as Guam, Wake Island, Hong Kong, and the Phillipines. America and its allies seemed helpless against the powerful Japanese military.

Finally, in May 1942, things began to change. At the battle of the Coral Sea, the Japanese fleet was prevented from landing troops in New Guinea. Although the fight was a draw, it was the first time the Japanese had not won a battle.

One month later, an important battle was fought near the U.S.-held Midway Island. In that battle, U.S. forces dealt a crippling blow to the Japanese fleet, sinking four aircraft carriers and shooting down many aircraft crews—and with it, the hopes of a Japanese victory in the Pacific. ■

THE FEARED U.S. CARRIERS

In the 1930s, Japan wanted to expand its borders by conquering nearby countries. To do this, Japan would have needed important natural resources, such as oil. The way to obtain these resources was through military muscle. But first, Japan had to prevent the United States from interfering with its plans. This meant destroying the American navy.

On December 7, 1941, aircraft from the Japanese Imperial Navy attacked Pearl Harbor, home of the U.S. Pacific Fleet and their warships. Six battleships were sunk or badly destroyed, three destroyers were ripped by bombs, three cruisers were damaged, and four other ships were sunk or damaged. Yet despite the vast destruction,

▲

The success of the surprise Japanese attack on US naval base Pearl Harbor led the Japanese to believe they were unstoppable against the Americans. (NARA)

the attack was not a total success for the Japanese. The American aircraft carriers that Japan feared were not in the harbor that day. The carriers escaped attack, and they were still a threat to the Japanese.

In the months immediately after Pearl Harbor, Japan defeated American and British forces time after time in the Pacific. It looked as if nothing could stop them. Then, on April 18, 1942, in one of the war's boldest and most surprising events, the Americans fought back. A group of B-25 bombers, launched from the U.S. aircraft carrier *Hornet,* bombed Tokyo, about 670 miles away. The raid did little damage but it was a huge surprise to the Japanese. The Japanese had thought they were unbeatable and that their country was safe from attack.

By early 1942, the Japanese were already beginning to plan an invasion of the U.S.-held island of Midway. The Japanese were worried that their mainland would soon be in range of U.S. aircraft carriers coming from nearby Hawaii. With the B-25 raid on Tokyo, the Japanese were convinced beyond any doubt: they were in danger. The Japanese needed to bring the American

After Japan declared war against America at Pearl Harbor, they began to invade and attack other islands, including Malaya in 1942. (Courtesy of the Robert Hunt Library)

▲

Japanese aircraft carrier *Hiryu* was the last carrier built by Japan before World War 2. The ship was constructed at Yokosuka Naval Yard. (Courtesy of Roger Chesneau)

carriers into battle and destroy them once and for all. Midway was to be that battle.

Planning for the Midway invasion was given to Japanese Admiral Isoroku Yamamoto. Because he had successfully planned the attack on Pearl Harbor, he was given complete control of the operation. Although the idea of invading Midway was simple, the plan itself was quite complicated.

The plan was split into two parts; they were called Operation AL and Operation MI. Operation AL was a trick to lure American forces to the north, away from Midway. To do this, a small Japanese force would attack the Aleutian Islands in Alaska.

Operation MI was the invasion of Midway itself and had a very strict timetable. The four main Japanese aircraft carriers were to launch air strikes against Midway to destroy the American aircraft there. They would then attack the U.S. carriers when they arrived in defense of the island. But it was the Japanese who were in for a surprise.

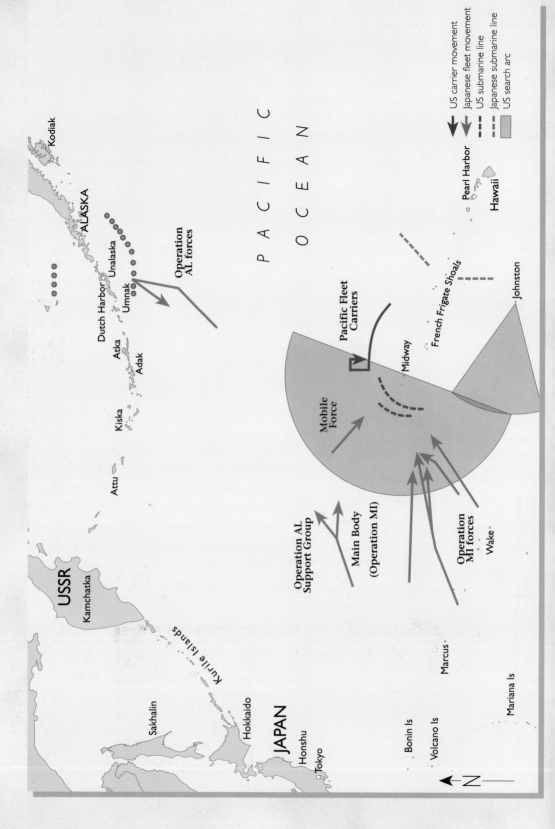

THE JAPANESE PLAN OF ATTACK

The invasion of Midway would take place on June 7, while the Japanese battleship fleet, called the Main Body, would lie in wait for the Americans. At the same time, Japanese scout planes and submarines would wait between Midway and Hawaii to warn the Japanese when the U.S. arrived.

Even with Yamamoto's careful planning, the Japanese faced problems. First, the strict plan made dealing with any surprises difficult. Secondly, the Japanese had little information on where the American ships were, especially the U.S. carriers. Despite this, Yamamoto was confident that America was unaware of his plan. He couldn't have been more wrong.

As far back as April 1942, the Americans knew of the attack on Midway. A team under Commander Joseph Rochefort had cracked

Commander Joseph Rochefort cracked Japanese Navy codes just before the battle of Midway, and was able to notify his fellow Americans of Japan's plan of attack. (US Navy)

LEFT The battle of Midway, which began on June 4, 1942, was a battle which became a fight between U.S. and Japanese aircraft carriers, the planes and their pilots. Their secret plan of attack on Midway discovered, the Japanese fleet lost the element of surprise, and were searched for, found, and destroyed by the Americans.

secret Japanese Navy communication codes and discovered their plan. Rochefort told U.S. Navy Pacific Commander, Admiral Chester Nimitz, who sent more forces to Midway.

He then ordered the carriers *Enterprise* and *Hornet* of Task Force (TF) 16 to head to Midway on May 28, under the command of Rear Admiral Raymond Spruance. They were to be joined by carrier *Yorktown* of TF 17, commanded by Rear Admiral Frank Fletcher.

Fortunately for the U.S., their carriers slipped past the Japanese unnoticed. Nimitz decided that the attack on the Aleutians was a decoy. He sent only 15 warships to defend the islands. His plan was to use Midway as a fourth unsinkable aircraft carrier. But he knew that many of the 115 planes based there were old and slow. His best chance was to use them and the carrier aircraft in a quick surprise, hit-and-run attack, to cause as much damage as possible.

To do this, he had to keep the location of his carriers a total secret. He didn't tell those at Midway that they were to be supported by the carriers. In fact, the Navy pilots were told they would be defending Pearl Harbor, not launching an attack against the Japanese fleet. Nimitz wanted to find them as soon as possible, so he could strike first.

Attacked at Midway by U.S. aircraft; B-17s and SBDs, Japanese carrier *Hiryu* tried desperately to avoid them, but without success. It sank after being hit by four bombs. (NARA)

BATTLE OF MIDWAY

JUNE 3, 1942, 3:00 A.M. THE OPENING MOVES OF THE BATTLE OF MIDWAY ARE MADE.

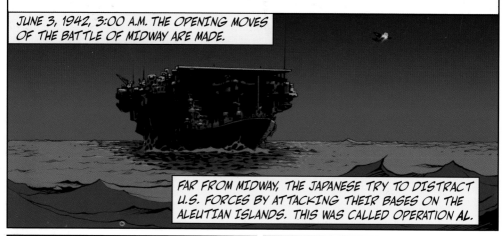

FAR FROM MIDWAY, THE JAPANESE TRY TO DISTRACT U.S. FORCES BY ATTACKING THEIR BASES ON THE ALEUTIAN ISLANDS. THIS WAS CALLED OPERATION AL.

THE JAPANESE CARRIERS *RYUJO* AND *JUNYO* LAUNCH ATTACKS AGAINST DUTCH HARBOR ON THE ALEUTIANS.

RYUJO'S AIRCRAFT ARE LUCKIER. THEY SPOT THE HARBOR THROUGH A GAP IN THE CLOUDS, BUT THEY ARE SEEN BY AMERICAN RADAR.

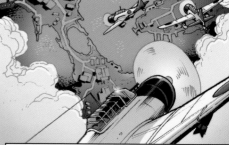

BUT JUNYO'S PLANES BECOME LOST IN FOG.

AT 8:08 A.M., THE JAPANESE AIRCRAFT START THEIR ATTACK.

U.S. ANTI-AIRCRAFT GUNS FROM DUTCH HARBOR AND *CURTISS P-40* FIGHTER PLANES GREET THE JAPANESE.

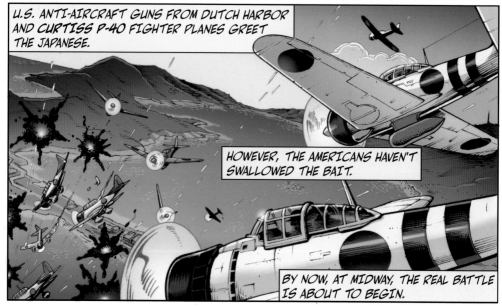

HOWEVER, THE AMERICANS HAVEN'T SWALLOWED THE BAIT.

BY NOW, AT MIDWAY, THE REAL BATTLE IS ABOUT TO BEGIN.

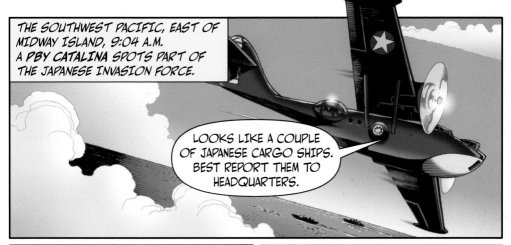

THE SOUTHWEST PACIFIC, EAST OF MIDWAY ISLAND, 9:04 A.M. A *PBY CATALINA* SPOTS PART OF THE JAPANESE INVASION FORCE.

LOOKS LIKE A COUPLE OF JAPANESE CARGO SHIPS. BEST REPORT THEM TO HEADQUARTERS.

9:25 A.M. ENSIGN JACK REID IS FLYING HIS PBY AT THE VERY LIMIT OF ITS RANGE. HE SEES A GROUP OF JAPANESE SHIPS ON THE HORIZON AND REPORTS BACK.

SIGHTED MAIN BODY! SIGHTED MAIN BODY!

REID'S HEADQUARTERS WANT AS MUCH DETAIL AS POSSIBLE.

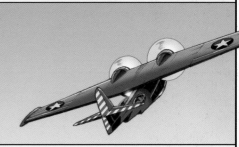

BUT THE SKY IS CLEAR AND WITHOUT ANY PROTECTIVE CLOUDS, SO REID HAS TO STALK THE JAPANESE SHIPS VERY CAREFULLY.

FINALLY, APPROACHING FROM BEHIND, REID CAN CLEARLY SEE THE FLEET OF SHIPS.

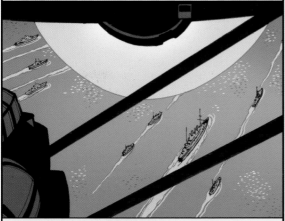

IT IS THE MIDWAY INVASION FORCE: TWO LINES OF TRANSPORT SHIPS PROTECTED BY DESTROYERS AND THE LIGHT CRUISER *JINTSU*.

HOWEVER, HAVING SEEN SO MANY DIFFERENT JAPANESE SHIPS, REID BECOMES CONFUSED. INSTEAD OF THE CORRECT INVASION FORCE, HE REPORTS...

LOOKS LIKE A SMALL CARRIER, TWO BATTLESHIPS, SEVERAL CRUISERS, AND VARIOUS OTHER SHIPS.

DESPITE REID'S MISTAKE, AMERICA NOW KNOWS A LARGE JAPANESE FORCE IS HEADING TOWARD MIDWAY.

JINTSU SPOTS REID'S PBY OVERHEAD...

ALL SHIPS, ALL SHIPS! AMERICAN SCOUT OVERHEAD!

THE JAPANESE COMMANDERS REALIZE THEY MAY BE GOING INTO BATTLE EARLIER THAN PLANNED.

12:25 P.M. AFTER REID'S REPORT, AMERICA PREPARES FOR BATTLE AND U.S. AIRCRAFT ARE ORDERED TO ATTACK.

ON MIDWAY ISLAND, NINE B-17 FLYING FORTRESSES TAKE OFF.

4:40 P.M. THE B-17S FINALLY ARRIVE OVER THE JAPANESE INVASION FORCE.

THE ESCORTING DESTROYERS AND JINTSU OPEN FIRE AT THE HIGHFLYING BOMBERS. THEY SCORE NO HITS.

THE B-17S ARE EQUALLY INACCURATE. DESPITE CLAIMS BY THEIR PILOTS OF HITTING SEVERAL SHIPS, NO BOMBS REACH THEIR TARGETS.

THE U.S. SUBMARINE CUTTLEFISH IS SENT TO FINISH OFF THE "VICTIMS" OF THE B-17 ATTACK.

UNSURPRISINGLY, IT DOESN'T FIND ANY.

U.S. ADMIRAL CHESTER NIMITZ AND REAR ADMIRAL FRANK FLETCHER DON'T BELIEVE THE JAPANESE CARRIERS SPOTTED BY REID ARE THE ONES THEY'RE AFTER.

I THINK THE ONES WE WANT WON'T SHOW UNTIL TOMORROW MORNING.

FLETCHER ORDERS THE CARRIERS OF TASK FORCE (TF) 16 AND 17 TO HEAD SOUTH THROUGH THE NIGHT, TO A POINT NORTH OF MIDWAY.

FROM HERE HE HOPES TO LAUNCH HIS AIRCRAFT AGAINST THE ARRIVING JAPANESE CARRIERS.

1:30 A.M., JUNE 4.

FOUR PBYS FROM MIDWAY, EACH FITTED TO CARRY A SINGLE TORPEDO, ATTACK THE INVASION FORCE SPOTTED BY REID.

ONE TORPEDO HITS THE OIL TANKER *AKEBONO MARU*. ALTHOUGH IT KILLS 11 SAILORS, DAMAGE IS LIGHT.

THE PBYS ESCAPE THROUGH A STORM OF ANTI-AIRCRAFT FIRE.

3:00 A.M. ABOARD CARRIERS *AKAGI*, *HIRYU*, *KAGA*, AND *SORYU* OF THE FIRST JAPANESE STRIKING FORCE, AIRCRAFT PREPARE TO ATTACK MIDWAY.

ARMED AND FUELED, WITH ENGINES WARMED UP, THE PLANES AWAIT THEIR PILOTS.

VICE ADMIRAL NAGUMO, COMMANDER OF THE FIRST AIR FLEET, CHOOSES LESS EXPERIENCED PILOTS FOR THE FIRST ATTACK WAVE.

HE KEEPS THE BETTER PILOTS BACK IN CASE THE AMERICAN CARRIERS APPEAR.

4:30 A.M. 36 MITSUBISHI A6M2 "ZERO" FIGHTER PLANES LAUNCH FROM *SORYU*.

THE ZEROES WAIT OVERHEAD WHILE THEY ARE JOINED BY *NAKAJIMA B5N "KATE"* AND *AICHI D3A "VAL"* BOMBERS FROM OTHER CARRIERS.

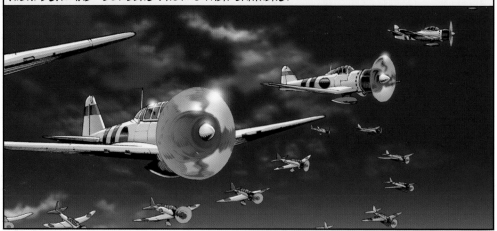

AT 4:45 A.M. THE FIRST WAVE OF 108 JAPANESE AIRCRAFT TURN SOUTHEAST TOWARD MIDWAY.

ONLY NINE ZEROES ARE LAUNCHED TO PROTECT THE ENTIRE JAPANESE FLEET. ANOTHER NINE ARE FUELED AND READY ON *AKAGI'S* DECK.

12

THE JAPANESE ALSO BEGIN TO LAUNCH THEIR SCOUT AIRCRAFT. A *NAKAJIMA E8N "DAVE"* IS FIRST IN THE AIR FROM BATTLESHIP *HARUNA.*

NEXT AWAY ARE THE NEW *YOKOSUKA D4Y "JUDY"* SCOUT PLANES FROM CARRIER *SORYU.*

BUT THE *MITSUBISHI TYPE 'O' "PETE"* FLOATPLANES ABOARD CRUISERS *CHIKUMA* AND *TOME* ARE HELD UP BY MECHANICAL PROBLEMS.

THEY ALL LAUNCH LATE.

THE JAPANESE PLAN OF ATTACK CALLS FOR SINGLE SCOUT PLANES TO PATROL THEIR OWN AREAS OVER THE SEA, IN SEARCH OF AMERICAN CARRIERS.

NO BOMBERS ARE ALLOWED TO JOIN THE SCOUTS SO THEY ARE THINLY SPREAD.

THE SCOUTS MUST REMAIN UNSEEN, SO AS NOT TO ALERT THE ENEMY.

13

4:00 A.M. MIDWAY ISLAND. MEANWHILE, THE AMERICANS ARE ALSO BUSY LAUNCHING AIRCRAFT.

16 B-17S FOLLOW THEM.

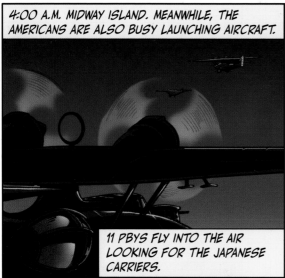

11 PBYS FLY INTO THE AIR LOOKING FOR THE JAPANESE CARRIERS.

5:20 A.M. LIEUTENANT HOWARD P. ADY'S PBY SPOTS A JAPANESE SPY PLANE.

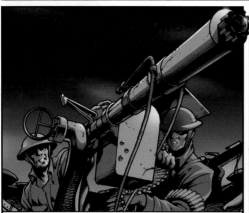

MIDWAY'S MARINES CLEAN AND ARM THEIR WEAPONS IN PREPARATION. RADARS SWEEP THE SKIES FOR ANY SIGN OF APPROACHING JAPANESE AIRCRAFT.

GOT A FLOATPLANE BELOW US -- COULD BE A DAVE OR A PETE!

5:30 A.M. ANOTHER PBY REPORTS IN.

5:50 A.M. ANOTHER PBY SPOTS THE JAPANESE AERIAL STRIKE FORCE APPROACHING MIDWAY.

THE AMERICANS NOW ALSO KNOW WHAT THE JAPANESE FIRST PLAN OF ATTACK IS: AN AERIAL ASSAULT...

CARRIER BEARING 320, DISTANCE 180!

IT'S THE REPORT THE AMERICANS ARE WAITING TO HEAR. NOW THEY KNOW WHERE THE JAPANESE CARRIERS ARE.

THE AMERICAN PBYS BEGIN TO PESTER THE JAPANESE.

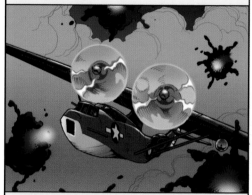

HEAVY ANTI-AIRCRAFT FIRE FROM THE JAPANESE SHIPS IS USED TO STOP THE SCOUTS.

ZEROES FROM CARRIER **KAGA** GO HUNTING FOR THE PBY CATALINAS BUT LOSE THEM IN THE CLOUDS.

THEN, AT 5:52 A.M., LT. ADY REPORTS EVEN MORE VITAL INFORMATION.

TWO CARRIERS AND BATTLESHIPS BEARING 320 DEGREES. DISTANCE 180, COURSE 135, SPEED 25!

THIS CONFIRMS THE EXACT POSITION OF THE JAPANESE SHIPS.

A MINUTE LATER, MIDWAY'S RADAR PICKS UP THE INCOMING JAPANESE AERIAL ATTACK.

MARINE CORPS **BREWSTER F2 BUFFALO** AND **GRUMAN F-4F WILDCAT** FIGHTERS SCRAMBLE TO MEET THEM.

NEXT INTO THE AIR ARE 16 MARINE **DOUGLAS TBD DEVASTATOR** DIVEBOMBERS.

MORE BOMBERS FOLLOW, INCLUDING THE MARINE **GRUMAN TBF AVENGERS** AND FOUR ARMY **MARTIN B-26 MARAUDERS**.

IT'S THE FIRST TIME IN COMBAT FOR THESE TWO PLANES.

ALL PLANES ARE IN THE AIR, WAITING FOR THE JAPANESE.

MEANWHILE, AT 6:00 A.M., THE B-17S THAT HAD LEFT TO ATTACK THE INVASION FLEET ARE SENT TO JOIN THE OTHER BOMBERS IN ATTACKING THE CARRIERS.

BUT THE STRIKE IS POORLY PLANNED. THERE IS NO FIGHTER COVER TO PROTECT THE BOMBERS.

THE BUFFALOES AND WILDCATS ARE OVER MIDWAY, WAITING FOR THE JAPANESE PLANES. AT 6:16 A.M., THEY ARRIVE.

HAVING THE ELEMENT OF SURPRISE, THE U.S. FIGHTERS ROLL INTO THE ATTACK, GUNS BLAZING.

YET THE ZEROES ARE FASTER AND MORE MANEUVERABLE THAN THE AMERICAN FIGHTERS. THE ZEROES GET IN BEHIND THEM AS THEY START THEIR ATTACK.

A DOGFIGHT ERUPTS. 13 BUFFALOES AND TWO WILDCATS ARE SHOT DOWN. THE JAPANESE LOSE THREE BOMBERS AND TWO ZEROES.

6:20 A.M. ON MIDWAY, FILMMAKER JOHN FORD, WHO WILL GO ON TO DIRECT A NUMBER OF FAMOUS WESTERNS, IS MAKING MOVIES FOR THE NAVY.

THEY'RE COMING!

HE IS ONE OF THE FIRST TO SPOT THE APPROACHING ATTACKERS.

WITH NO AIRCRAFT TO BOMB, KATES ATTACK THE OIL TANKS ON THE ISLAND. THE TANKS BURST INTO FLAMES.

VAL DIVEBOMBERS BLAST THE EMPTY HANGARS AND OTHER BUILDINGS.

ZEROES, NEWLY RELEASED FROM ESCORT DUTY, STRAFE THE ISLAND.

JEEZ! LOOK AT THAT IDIOT!

STRANGELY, ONE OF THEM FLIES UPSIDE DOWN ALONG MIDWAY'S RUNWAY. IT IS QUICKLY SHOT DOWN.

THE ISLAND'S ANTI-AIRCRAFT GUNS POUR FIRE AT THE ATTACKING PLANES.

THEY ARE JOINED BY PT BOATS JUST OFFSHORE.

6:43 A.M. THE JAPANESE AIRCRAFT HEAD OFF, LEAVING THE ISLAND BURNING.

BUT THE ATTACK HAS BEEN A FAILURE. MIDWAY'S RUNWAYS ARE UNDAMAGED. THE ISLAND REMAINS A THREAT TO THE JAPANESE.

EARLIER, AT 4:30 A.M. ...

AS *SORYU* LAUNCHES HER ZEROES, 220 MILES AWAY FROM THE AMERICAN FLEET, 10 DEVASTATORS ARE FLYING FROM CARRIER USS *YORKTOWN*.

THEY TURN NORTH TO SCOUT FOR POSSIBLE JAPANESE CARRIERS.

U.S. INTELLIGENCE REPORTS NAGUMO'S CARRIERS ARE TO THE NORTHWEST. BUT ADMIRAL FLETCHER, ABOARD *YORKTOWN*, DOESN'T WANT TO BE TAKEN BY SURPRISE.

WHEN LT. ADY'S PBY SPOTS THE TWO JAPANESE CARRIERS AT 5:30 A.M., FLETCHER IS MORE CERTAIN OF WHERE THE JAPANESE ARE.

THEN WORD ARRIVES LATER OF THE STRIKE ON MIDWAY.

THE TIME DELAY MUST MEAN NAGUMO'S FLEET IS ABOUT 200 MILES AWAY!

TF 16 COMMANDER, REAR ADMIRAL RAYMOND SPRUANCE, HAD PLANNED FOR CARRIERS USS *ENTERPRISE* AND USS *HORNET* TO BE WITHIN 100 MILES OF THE JAPANESE BEFORE LAUNCHING HIS ATTACK.

NOW THAT HE KNOWS THE JAPANESE LOCATION, HE PREDICTS MIDWAY'S ATTACKERS WILL BE BACK ABOARD THEIR CARRIERS AT AROUND 9:00 A.M. AND PRIME TARGETS.

HOWEVER, TO CATCH THE PLANES ON DECK, SPRUANCE WILL HAVE TO LAUNCH TWO HOURS EARLIER THAN PLANNED.

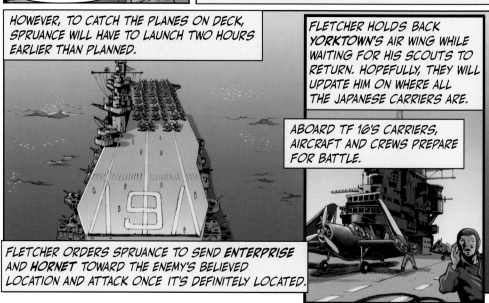

FLETCHER ORDERS SPRUANCE TO SEND *ENTERPRISE* AND *HORNET* TOWARD THE ENEMY'S BELIEVED LOCATION AND ATTACK ONCE IT'S DEFINITELY LOCATED.

FLETCHER HOLDS BACK *YORKTOWN'S* AIR WING WHILE WAITING FOR HIS SCOUTS TO RETURN. HOPEFULLY, THEY WILL UPDATE HIM ON WHERE ALL THE JAPANESE CARRIERS ARE.

ABOARD TF 16'S CARRIERS, AIRCRAFT AND CREWS PREPARE FOR BATTLE.

7:00 A.M. **HORNET** STARTS LAUNCHING 60 AIRCRAFT.

THERE ARE 15 DOUGLAS TBD **DEVASTATORS** AND 35 SBD **DAUNTLESS** DIVEBOMBERS.

10 WILDCATS FLY ABOVE THEM FOR COVER.

ENTERPRISE'S SBDS AND TBDS JOIN THEM.

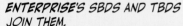

YORKTOWN'S SCOUTS RETURN.

D'YOU FIND THE REST OF 'EM?

NOPE. JUST SAW THE TWO.

FLETCHER DECIDES THAT EVEN TWO JAPANESE CARRIERS IS A TEMPTING TARGET. HE LAUNCHES HALF HIS AIR WING.

SPRUANCE HAS KEPT BACK 36 WILDCATS TO COVER THE CARRIERS.

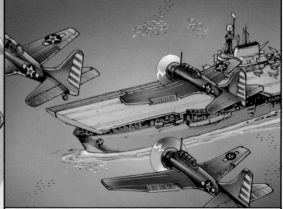

BY 9:10 A.M., 156 U.S. CARRIER AIRCRAFT ARE HEADING TOWARD THE JAPANESE.

ABOARD THE JAPANESE CARRIERS, 108 AIRCRAFT ARE WAITING FOR ORDERS TO ATTACK THE AMERICAN CARRIERS.

AT 7:00 A.M., NAGUMO RECEIVES A REQUEST TO ATTACK MIDWAY AGAIN.

NAGUMO HAS HIS MIND MADE UP FOR HIM WHEN MIDWAY-BASED AVENGERS AND B-26S ARE SPOTTED APPROACHING HIS FLEET.

HE ORDERS HIS ZEROES TO ATTACK THE U.S. PLANES.

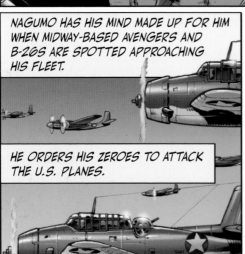

FLYING JUST ABOVE THE WAVES WITH THEIR BOMB DOORS OPEN, THE U.S. TORPEDO BOMBERS ARE SLOW.

ZEROES! ZEROES BEHIND US!

ZEROES QUICKLY CLOSE IN ON THEM.

THE U.S. BOMBERS ARE EASY PREY FOR THE SPEEDY ZEROES. FIVE ARE SHOT DOWN. THE BADLY DAMAGED SURVIVORS BARELY MAKE IT BACK TO MIDWAY.

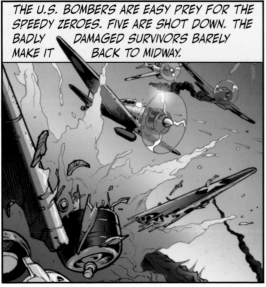

THE B-26S DO JUST AS POORLY. TWO ARE SHOT DOWN. ONE ALMOST COLLIDES WITH *AKAGI*.

THE OTHER TWO LAUNCH THEIR TORPEDOES AND RUN FOR IT. THEY SCORE NO HITS.

NAGUMO DECIDES TO SEND A SECOND WAVE OF PLANES TO MIDWAY.

ON THE JAPANESE CARRIERS, CREWMEN QUICKLY UNLOAD TORPEDOES FROM THE KATES AND REPLACE THEM WITH BOMBS.

THEN, JAPANESE CRUISER TONE'S SCOUT PLANE SPOTS 10 AMERICAN SHIPS IN THE DISTANCE. NAGUMO STILL DECIDES TO CONTINUE WITH THE STRIKE ON MIDWAY.

NAGUMO ALSO NEEDS TO PREPARE THE CARRIERS FOR OTHER AIRCRAFT RETURNING FROM THE FIRST MIDWAY ATTACK.

7:48 A.M. SUDDENLY, OUT OF NOWHERE, 16 SBDS ATTACK THE JAPANESE FLEET. HOWEVER, THE PILOTS HAVE LITTLE TRAINING AND THEY SUFFER BADLY.

BULLDOZED BY DEFENDING ZEROES, EIGHT SBDS ARE SHOT DOWN BEFORE THEY DROP THEIR BOMBS.

SURVIVING SBDS DROP THEIR BOMBS ON **HIRYU** BUT SCORE NO DIRECT HITS.

ESCAPING LOW ACROSS THE WAVES, THE DAUNTLESSES ARE CHASED BY MORE ZEROES.

FOUR MILES ABOVE, MIDWAY'S B-17S COME TO THE RESCUE AND BEGIN DROPPING THEIR BOMBS.

THE BOMBS MAKE HUGE SPLASHES BUT STILL HIT NOTHING.

8:06 A.M. NOW ABLE TO SEE MORE CLEARLY, JAPANESE *TONE'S* SCOUT REPORTS FIVE CRUISERS AND FIVE DESTROYERS.

EVEN THOUGH THEY SEE NO CARRIERS, THE JAPANESE ADMIRALS CAN'T BELIEVE THERE AREN'T ANY.

8:20 A.M. HOWEVER, THE FAILURE OF THE AMERICANS TO DO ANY DAMAGE TO THEIR CARRIERS LEAVES THE JAPANESE WITH LITTLE TO FEAR.

ANOTHER TOTALLY UNSUCCESSFUL ATTACK BY MIDWAY-BASED *SB2U VINDICATORS* FURTHER PROVES THE POINT.

8:30 A.M. AS THE PLANES OF THE FIRST MIDWAY ATTACK RETURN, *TONE'S* SCOUT FINALLY REPORTS AMERICAN CARRIERS.

SHOULD NAGUMO HAVE THE KATES REARMED WITH TORPEDOES TO ATTACK MIDWAY, OR SHOULD HE SEND THEM TO ATTACK THE CARRIERS WITH BOMBS?

ALSO, HIS FIGHTERS ARE NOW SHORT ON FUEL. IF THEY ARE TO ESCORT THE BOMBERS FOR A CARRIER ATTACK, THEY WILL NEED TO REFUEL.

BUT WHAT IF THE REPORT OF U.S. CARRIERS TURNS OUT TO BE FALSE?

8:35 A.M. NAGUMO DECIDES TO ATTACK THE CARRIERS.

THE KATES RETURN TO THE HANGAR DECKS TO RECEIVE THEIR TORPEDOES.

8:37 A.M. AS THE CARRIER PLANES LAND, THEY ARE QUICKLY REFUELED AND REARMED FOR THE COMING ATTACK.

8:45 A.M. *TONE'S* SCOUT IS LOW ON FUEL AND WANTS TO RETURN.

IT IS TOLD TO WAIT SO ITS RADIO SIGNAL CAN BE FOLLOWED TO THE AMERICANS.

9:17 A.M. THE JAPANESE FLEET TURNS NORTH TO CLOSE THE DISTANCE WITH THE AMERICANS. THEIR AIRCRAFT WILL BE READY TO LAUNCH BY 10:30 A.M.

9:20 A.M. A SHARP-EYED LOOKOUT ON CRUISER *CHIKUMA* SPOTS APPROACHING AIRCRAFT.

THERE ARE MASSES OF THEM! THEY'VE COME FOR US AT THE WORST POSSIBLE MOMENT!

THE U.S. PLAN OF ATTACK HAD BEEN THAT ALL CARRIER AIRCRAFT ARRIVE TOGETHER.

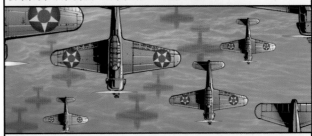

BUT, AFTER THE JAPANESE SCOUT PLANE IS SPOTTED, AND FEARING THE LOSS OF SURPRISE, 33 SBDS WERE SENT ON ALONE.

AROUND 8:00 A.M., MORE SBDS, WITH WILDCATS ESCORTING THEM OVERHEAD, WERE SENT TOWARD THE BELIEVED JAPANESE POSITION.

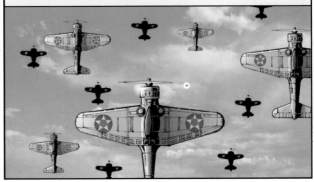

BELOW THEM, TWO SQUADRONS OF TBD DEVASTATORS FOLLOW. THE WILDCATS ARE SUPPOSED TO BE COVERING THEM TOO.

HOWEVER, THE WILDCATS BECOME SEPARATED FROM THE TBDS IN THE CLOUDS.

THE AMERICANS ARE STILL UNAWARE OF JAPAN'S SUDDEN CHANGE OF COURSE. THE SBDS AND WILDCATS CONTINUE SOUTH BUT FIND ONLY EMPTY OCEAN.

THE TBD DEVASTATORS OF NAVAL SQUADRON VT-8 ARE LED BY LIEUTENANT COMMANDER JOHN C. WALDON.

WALDON BELIEVES THE JAPANESE MUST BE AWARE OF THE AMERICAN CARRIERS BY NOW. HE FIGURES THEY WOULD CHANGE THEIR COURSE TO GO AFTER THEM. HE PLAYS HIS HUNCH.

INSTEAD OF FOLLOWING THE COURSE THE OTHER SQUADRONS TAKE, WALDON HEADS NORTH. HIS HUNCH IS RIGHT. AT 9:20 A.M., THE JAPANESE FLEET COMES INTO VIEW.

VT-8! THERE THEY ARE! START YOUR ATTACK!

AS MANY AS 50 ZEROES ARE COVERING THE FLEET. THEY CHARGE AT THE TBDS.

ZEROES! LOADS OF 'EM! COMING DOWN NOW!

THE LOST WILDCATS ARE 20,000 FEET OVERHEAD. THEY ARE UNAWARE OF THE VT-8'S PLIGHT.

WALDON DOESN'T KNOW THE SIGNAL NEEDED TO BRING THEM TO THEIR AID.

WITH FIGHTER COVER CIRCLING UNAWARE OVERHEAD, VT-8 LOSES FOUR AIRCRAFT IN SECONDS.

IN THE COCKPIT OF HIS TBD, ENSIGN GEORGE GAY OPENS FIRE AT A ZERO THAT FLASHES PAST IN FRONT OF HIM.

I GOT HIM, I GOT HIM!

THE TBD'S SINGLE MACHINE GUN DOES LITTLE DAMAGE BUT MAKES GAY FEEL A LOT BETTER.

AS GAY STARTS TOWARD **AKAGI**, HIS DEVASTATOR IS SURROUNDED BY A STORM OF ANTI-AIRCRAFT FIRE FROM THE SHIPS.

A SHELL EXPLODES AT HIS FEET, BURNING HIS RIGHT LEG. HE HAS BULLET WOUNDS IN HIS LEFT HAND AND ARM.

AAIIIHHHH!

GAY QUICKLY RELEASES HIS TORPEDO AT **AKAGI**, BUT IT MISSES.

GAY PULLS UP AND OVER **AKAGI**, ALMOST HITTING ITS ISLAND.

AS GAY TRIES TO ESCAPE, A LINE OF ZEROES PULL IN BEHIND HIM. ONE OF THEM SHOOTS OUT HIS RUDDER.

GAY'S BATTERED TBD FINALLY CRASHES INTO THE SEA.

THE CRASH BENDS GAY'S COCKPIT. HE HAS TO FIGHT TO GET IT OPEN.

HE THEN SWIMS DOWN TO TRY TO RESCUE HIS GUNNER FROM THE SINKING PLANE, BUT IT'S TOO LATE.

ALL 15 TBDS OF VT-8 ARE SHOT DOWN. GAY IS THE ONLY SURVIVOR.

HE IS PICKED UP THE FOLLOWING DAY BY A PBY. HE WITNESSES THE ENTIRE BATTLE OF MIDWAY FROM THE WAVES.

FOLLOWING THE ATTACK, THE JAPANESE STILL NEED SOME TIME TO FINISH READYING THEIR STRIKE AGAINST THE AMERICAN CARRIERS.

THEN 14 MORE TBDS OF SQUADRON VT-6 ARRIVE.

THEY BECOME MORE EASY TARGETS FOR THE ZEROES.

ONLY SEVEN TBDS SURVIVE TO RELEASE THEIR TORPEDOES AT **HIRYU**.

THE CARRIER TURNS HARD TO PORT. IT AVOIDS ALL THE TORPEDOES.

THREE MORE TBDS ARE SHOT DOWN. ONLY FOUR MAKE IT BACK TO **ENTERPRISE**.

BY NOW THE ZEROES ARE LOW ON FUEL AND ARE LANDING TO REFILL THEIR TANKS.

THE PILOTS ALSO TAKE THE OPPORTUNITY TO REFUEL.

THEN, AT 10:15 A.M., THE TBD DEVASTATORS OF NAVY SQUADRON VT-3 ARRIVE.

THEY HAD SET OUT FROM *YORKTOWN*, WITH AN ESCORT OF WILDCATS AND 17 SBD DAUNTLESSES OVERHEAD.

BUT AS THEY STARTED TOWARD THEIR TARGET, THE HIGHFLYING SBDS BECAME SEPARATED FROM THE OTHERS.

I LOST 'EM! CAN'T SEE THEM THROUGH THESE CLOUDS!

AS THE TBD TORPEDO BOMBERS START THEIR APPROACH, THEIR FIGHTER COVER IS BOMBARDED BY ZEROES. THE WILDCATS ARE SOON FIGHTING FOR THEIR LIVES.

THE TBD ATTACK IS A RERUN OF PREVIOUS TORPEDO BOMBER ATTEMPTS.

FIVE ARE SHOT DOWN BY ZEROES AS THEY START THEIR APPROACH.

FIVE MANAGE TO LAUNCH TORPEDOES AT *AKAGI* AND *KAGA*. BUT THEY SCORE NO HITS.

BY THE END OF THE ATTACK ONLY TWO TBDS ARE LEFT.

10:20 A.M. THE JAPANESE ARE VERY PLEASED. ANOTHER AMERICAN ATTACK HAS BEEN SHOT TO PIECES.

THE TIME HAS COME TO LAUNCH THEIR STRIKE.

BUT THE TBDS AND THEIR MEN HAVE NOT BEEN LOST IN VAIN.

THEIR ATTACKS HAVE PREVENTED THE JAPANESE STRIKE FROM BEING LAUNCHED. IT HAS ALSO BROUGHT THEIR ZEROES DOWN TO SEA LEVEL.

HAVING LOST THE OTHERS FROM **YORKTOWN**, THE SBDS OF NAVY SQUADRON VB-3, UNDER LT. COMMANDER MAXWELL F. LESLIE, AT LAST FIND THE   JAPANESE.

THEY HAVE BEEN JOINED BY THE 33 SBDS FROM CARRIER **ENTERPRISE**, UNDER LT. COMMANDER WADE McCLUSKY.

McCLUSKY HAD BEEN UNABLE TO FIND THE JAPANESE WHEN THEY CHANGED COURSE. HOWEVER, HE ALSO DECIDED TO TRY HIS LUCK TO THE NORTH.

SPOTTING THE WAKE LEFT BY A JAPANESE DESTROYER, HE FINALLY FOUND THE JAPANESE FLEET.

LT. COMMANDER LESLIE WAS ALSO HAVING SOME PROBLEMS.

OH *$@#!

FAULTY ELECTRONICS CAUSED SOME SBDS TO SUDDENLY DROP THEIR BOMBS.

THE TWO SQUADRONS ARE APPROACHING FROM TWO DIFFERENT DIRECTIONS.

AT 10:20 A.M., THEY BEGIN THEIR DIVES.

THE SBDS LIVE UP TO THEIR "HELLDIVER" NICKNAME AS THEY HURTLE DOWN FROM THE CLOUDS.

WOW! THERE ARE FOUR -- NOT TWO -- CARRIERS!

THE FIRST HIT IS **KAGA**, PERHAPS BECAUSE IT IS THE BIGGEST.

A BOMB HITS THE AIRCRAFT PACKED TOGETHER ON THE CARRIER'S FLIGHT DECK.

MORE BOMBS HIT HOME. BURNING FUEL TURNS THE MIGHTY **KAGA** INTO AN INFERNO. 800 CREWMEN, INCLUDING THE CAPTAIN, ARE KILLED.

THE CARRIER FINALLY SINKS AT 7:25 P.M., WHEN ITS AMMUNITION MAGAZINES EXPLODE.

AKAGI IS NEXT. A BOMB HITS THE MIDDLE OF THE SHIP, CAUSING MAYHEM.

AS ON ALL THE JAPANESE CARRIERS, AKAGI'S AIRCRAFT ARE FULLY LOADED WITH FUEL AND AMMO.

THE NEXT BOMB LANDS AMONG THEM. ONE EXPLOSION BECOMES MANY AS FUEL, BOMBS, AND TORPEDOES EXPLODE IN THE FIRE.

THE PILOTS, SITTING IN THE PLANES READY FOR TAKE OFF, DIE IN THEIR COCKPITS.

AAAAAAAIIIIIHHH!

WHEN THE FIRE REACHES THE HANGAR DECK BELOW, EVEN MORE FUEL AND BOMBS EXPLODE.

WITH AKAGI IN RUINS, NAGUMO ESCAPES TO THE CRUISER, NAGARA.

TO LEAVE THE CARRIER, HE HAS TO CLIMB DOWN A ROPE FROM A WINDOW ON THE SHIP'S ISLAND BECAUSE FIRE HAS CUT OFF HIS ESCAPE ROUTE.

AKAGI STAYS AFLOAT UNTIL DAWN THE NEXT DAY. IT IS THEN TORPEDOED BY JAPANESE DESTROYERS, ENDING ITS MISERY.

ALMOST 300 MEN HAVE BEEN KILLED.

10:25 A.M. A TRIO OF SBDS ATTACK CARRIER *SORYU*.

DIVEBOMBERS! NO!!

THREE BOMBS HIT THE FLIGHT DECK, ONE PASSING THROUGH IT INTO THE HANGAR.

GREAT HIT! GREAT HIT!

IT EXPLODES AMONGST THE AIRCRAFT PARKED THERE.

THE FIREBALL IT CREATES IS SO FIERCE IT BLASTS THE FORWARD ELEVATOR INTO THE AIR.

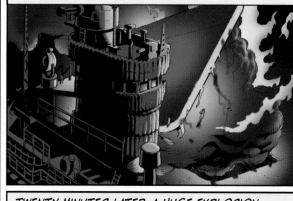

TWENTY MINUTES LATER, A HUGE EXPLOSION THROWS MEN INTO THE WATER.

SEEING ALL HOPE IS LOST, CAPTAIN YANAGIMOTO GIVES THE ORDER TO ABANDON HIS SHIP. DESTROYERS MOVE IN TO PICK UP SURVIVORS.

STILL ABOARD WHEN *SORYU* FINALLY SINKS AT 7:13 P.M., YANAGIMOTO IS ONE OF THE 718 MEN WHO GO DOWN WITH THE SHIP.

WITH THREE OF HIS CARRIERS DESTROYED, NAGUMO HANDS COMMAND OVER TO REAR ADMIRAL ABE HIRAOKI BELIEVING HE IS NO LONGER FIT TO COMMAND. HIRAOKI ISSUES HIS FIRST ORDER...

TELL *HIRYU* TO LAUNCH A STRIKE AGAINST THE AMERICAN CARRIERS!

AT 10:58 A.M., THE FIRST WAVE OF 18 VALS AND SIX ZEROES TAKE OFF FROM *HIRYU*.

THEY ARE GUIDED TO THE AMERICANS BY RADIO REPORTS FROM *TONE'S* SCOUT PLANE, WHO IS STILL WATCHING THEM.

NOON: THE JAPANESE ARE PICKED UP BY *YORKTOWN'S* RADAR JUST AS IT IS PREPARING TO RECOVER THE SBD "HELLDIVERS."

THEY HAVE TO WAIT WHILE 15 WILDCATS ARE LAUNCHED IN DEFENSE.

THEY JOIN 12 OTHERS ALREADY AIRBORNE.

MORE WILDCATS ARRIVE FROM OTHER CARRIERS. THERE ARE NOW 28 WILDCATS WAITING TO GREET THE JAPANESE.

AS THEY APPROACH, VALS ARE BOMBARDED BY THE WILDCATS, WHO IMMEDIATELY SHOOT DOWN 10.

THREE MORE ARE DOWNED BY ANTI-AIRCRAFT FIRE FROM THE AMERICAN FLEET.

THREE VALS MANAGE TO DROP THEIR BOMBS ON *YORKTOWN*. ONE HITS THE ISLAND. ANOTHER EXPLODES ON THE FLIGHT DECK.

TWO VALS ARE SHOT DOWN.

THE THIRD BOMB PASSES THROUGH THE FORWARD ELEVATOR. IT EXPLODES IN THE HANGAR BELOW THE FLIGHT DECK.

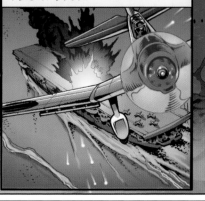

WITH *YORKTOWN* IN DANGER, ADMIRAL FLETCHER MOVES TO THE CRUISER *ASTORIA*.

THOUGH BADLY DAMAGED, *YORKTOWN* IS RAPIDLY REPAIRED.

10:40 P.M. FIGHTERS RETURN FOR REFUELING TO MEET THE EXPECTED RETURN OF THE JAPANESE.

MEANWHILE, WITH *SORYU* DESTROYED, ITS JUDY SCOUT PLANES HAVE LANDED ABOARD *HIRYU.*

CAPTAIN YAMAGUCHI LEARNS FROM THE SCOUTS THERE ARE THREE AMERICAN CARRIERS, NOT TWO.

1:31 P.M. CAPTAIN YAMAGUCHI IMMEDIATELY ORDERS A SECOND WAVE OF PLANES INTO THE AIR.

THERE ARE FEW AIRCRAFT LEFT -- JUST 10 KATES ESCORTED BY SIX ZEROES.

THE JAPANESE ARRIVE AT 2:30 P.M. CREWS HAVE BEEN WRONGLY TOLD THE *YORKTOWN* IS A BLAZING WRECK.

WILDCATS MEET THE JAPANESE, SHOOTING DOWN FIVE KATES.

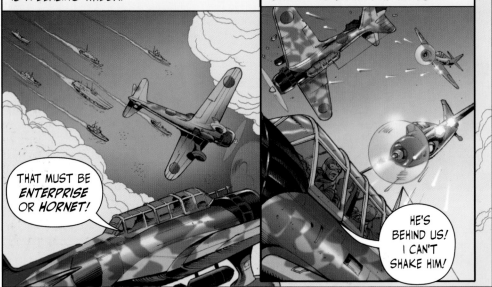

THAT MUST BE *ENTERPRISE* OR *HORNET!*

HE'S BEHIND US! I CAN'T SHAKE HIM!

ANOTHER IS SHOT DOWN AS THE SURVIVORS MAKE THEIR ATTACK RUNS. FOUR KATES MANAGE TO LAUNCH THEIR TORPEDOES.

TURNING HARD, *YORKTOWN* MANAGES TO AVOID TWO OF THE TORPEDOES.

THE OTHER TWO HIT *YORKTOWN* JUST 60 FEET APART. THEY CUT ALL POWER AND BRING THE   CARRIER TO A SUDDEN STOP.

IT QUICKLY BEGINS TO LIST TO THE LEFT.

3:00 P.M. THE ORDER IS GIVEN TO ABANDON SHIP. FOUR DESTROYERS RESCUE 2,270 MEMBERS OF YORKTOWN'S CREW.

IT CAN ONLY BE A MATTER OF TIME BEFORE *YORKTOWN* SINKS.

HELP ME! HELP ME, PLEASE!

35

AS THE SURVIVORS OF **HIRYU'S** FIRST STRIKE FORCE RETURN, THEY ARE SEEN BY LT. WALLACE SHORT IN HIS LONE SBD, 100 MILES NORTHWEST OF **YORKTOWN.**

THERE SHE IS! WE FOUND HER!

HEARING SHORT'S REPORT, SPRUANCE IMMEDIATELY ORDERS AN ATTACK ON **HIRYU.**

24 SBDS FROM **ENTERPRISE** AND 16 FROM **HORNET** LAUNCH AT 3:30 P.M. THERE IS NO FIGHTER COVER. THE FEW WILDCATS LEFT ARE PROTECTING THE U.S. CARRIERS.

4:30 P.M. THE LAST ARRIVE BACK AT **HIRYU.** THEY ARE MISTAKENLY CONVINCED THEY HAVE SUNK ANOTHER U.S. CARRIER.

WE DID IT! WE SANK THE **ENTERPRISE!**

YAMAGUCHI NOW BELIEVES HE CAN SNATCH VICTORY FROM TOTAL DEFEAT. HE ORDERS A THIRD STRIKE AT DUSK.

HOWEVER, ONLY 15 PLANES ARE LEFT FOR THE ATTACK, AND THEIR CREWS ARE EXHAUSTED.

AS THEIR PLANES ARE READIED FOR ACTION, THE CREWS QUICKLY ENJOY A MEAL OF SWEET RICE BALLS.

THE AMERICANS TAKE THE JAPANESE DEFENSES BY TOTAL SURPRISE.

HIRYU TURNS ALMOST A COMPLETE CIRCLE, ESCAPING THREE BOMBS.

HOWEVER, FOUR MORE SMASH INTO THE FLIGHT DECK. HUGE EXPLOSIONS TEAR OPEN THE FRONT OF THE SHIP.

IT IS TOTAL CARNAGE.

MANY OF THE CREW ARE KILLED IN THE BOMB BLASTS. OTHERS CHOKE ON THE THICK OIL SMOKE FROM FUEL FIRES.

HAK-HAK! GAK!

ANOTHER BOMB HITS THE FEW AIRCRAFT PARKED ON DECK. BURNING FUEL EXPLODES EVERYWHERE.

WITH THE CARRIER CRIPPLED, THE DAUNTLESSES TURN THEIR ATTENTION TO OTHER JAPANESE SHIPS.

HARUMA, TONE, AND CHIKUMA ARE ATTACKED BUT ESCAPE UNDAMAGED.

AS THE SBDS DEPART, THE FIGHT BEGINS TO SAVE HIRYU.

BUT WITH ALL HER FIREFIGHTING GEAR DESTROYED, OTHER SHIPS TRY HOSING SEAWATER ONTO THE FIRES.

THE DAMAGE IS TOO GREAT. THE SHIP SOON STARTS TO SINK.

SHE'S GOING OVER! HELP THE WOUNDED -- GET THEM OVER THE SIDE!

THERE'S ANOTHER BIG EXPLOSION AT 1:58 A.M.

ORDER ALL CREW TO ABANDON SHIP! NOW!

I SHALL REMAIN ABOARD!

BUT, SIR...

DESTROYER MAKIGUMO IS ORDERED TO FINISH OFF HIRYU WITH TORPEDOES. EVEN THEN, THE CARRIER REFUSES TO SINK.

FINALLY, **HIRYU** SINKS AT 8:20 A.M. ON JUNE 5. CAPTAIN YAMAGUCHI AND 416 MEN GO DOWN WITH THE SHIP.

MEANWHILE, **ADMIRAL YAMAMOTO** RECEIVES NEWS OF THE GROWING DISASTER AT 10:50 A.M ON JUNE 4.

ADMIRAL, THE REPORT READS, "FIRES RAGING ABOARD **KAGA**, **SORYU**, AND **AKAGI**."

NOOOOO... WHAT HAVE I DONE...?

YAMAMOTO ENDS OPERATION **AL** AND ORDERS CARRIERS **JUNYO** AND **RYUJO** SOUTH TO MIDWAY.

HE PLANS TO CRUSH THE AMERICANS BY BRINGING HIS FORCES TOGETHER WHEN THE CARRIERS ARRIVE ON JUNE 6.

HE THEN SENDS FOUR HEAVY CRUISERS TO MIDWAY, TO BOMBARD THE ISLAND.

BUT AT AROUND 5:00 P.M. HE LEARNS **HIRYU** HAS BEEN LOST.

7:07 P.M. AT SUNSET ON JUNE 4, AIRCRAFT THAT SANK *HIRYU* ARE RETURNING TO THEIR CARRIERS.

BY 7:20 P.M., THE LAST OF THE WILDCATS ARE ABOARD. SPRUANCE THEN ORDERS TF-16 TO WITHDRAW TO THE EAST.

WHEN YAMAMOTO HEARS THE AMERICANS ARE WITHDRAWING, HE REALIZES HIS CHANCE TO FIGHT BACK IS SLIPPING AWAY.

THEN, AT 9:30 P.M., NAGUMO TELLS YAMAMOTO HE WILL NOT JOIN HIM IN BATTLE. YAMAMOTO REPLACES HIM WITH ADMIRAL KONDO, WHO IS MORE WILLING TO FIGHT.

1:30 A.M. REVENGE BEGINS. JAPANESE SUBMARINE *I-168* SHELLS MIDWAY.

2:00 A.M. THE U.S. CARRIERS RETURN WEST TOWARD THE JAPANESE. THEY EXPECT MORE FIGHTING AT FIRST LIGHT.

JUNE 5. EARLY IN THE DAY, YORKTOWN IS STILL AFLOAT.

THE DECISION IS MADE TO TOW IT TO PEARL HARBOR. BUT THE CARRIER IS SPOTTED BY A JAPANESE SPY PLANE.

THIS SIGHTING IS RELAYED TO SUBMARINE *I-168*. THE SUB STALKS YORKTOWN THROUGH THE NIGHT AND SLIPS PAST THE SHIP'S ESCORTS.

AT 1:00 P.M. ON JUNE 6, THE SUB LAUNCHES FOUR TORPEDOES AT THE CARRIER.

ESCORT DESTROYER HAMMAN IS ALONGSIDE YORKTOWN.

HAMMAN IS HIT BY A TORPEDO. THE SHIP SPLITS IN TWO AND SINKS IMMEDIATELY.

AS THE DESTROYER SINKS, ITS DEPTH CHARGES EXPLODE. MANY OF THE CREW STRUGGLING IN THE WATER ARE KILLED.

TWO TORPEDOES PASS UNDER THE HAMMAN AND HIT YORKTOWN.

THE CARRIER IS NOW BEYOND SAVING, BUT IT SURVIVES THE NIGHT.

FINALLY, AT 4:58 A.M., JUNE 7, YORKTOWN SLIPS BENEATH THE WAVES.

MEANWHILE, AT 2:55 A.M. ON JUNE 5, IT IS CLEAR THAT THE JAPANESE FLEET HEADING TOWARD MIDWAY WON'T GET INTO ACTION UNTIL AT LEAST 3:00 A.M.

YAMAMOTO IS WORRIED THAT HIS SHIPS WILL BE OPEN TO ATTACK WHEN THE SUN RISES AT 4:00 A.M.

I HAVE LOST ENOUGH. CANCEL OPERATIONS AND ORDER ALL SHIPS TO WITHDRAW TO THE WEST!

MOST OF THE JAPANESE FLEET MEET BY 7:00 A.M. THEY ARE TO BE JOINED BY WHAT'S LEFT OF THE FIRST AIR FLEET AT MIDWAY ON JUNE 5.

THE CARNAGE, HOWEVER, IS NOT QUITE OVER.

EARLIER THAT MORNING, AT 1:18 A.M. AS FOUR HEAVY CRUISERS WERE HEADING TO ATTACK MIDWAY, AN AMERICAN SUB IS SPOTTED IN THE WATER.

PANICKING, CRUISER MOGAMI MAKES AN EMERGENCY TURN AND RAMS ANOTHER CRUISER, MIKUMA.

DAMAGE TO BOTH SHIPS IS BAD. MOGAMI'S BOW IS BENT COMPLETELY BACKWARD.

THE AMERICAN SUB DISAPPEARS.

MOGAMI AND MIKUMA ARE LEFT TO BE ESCORTED BY TWO DESTROYERS. THE REST OF THE CRUISERS HEAD OFF TO MEET THE FLEET.

6:30 A.M. A PBY DISCOVERS THEM AFTER FOLLOWING THE OIL TRAIL LEFT BY MIKUMA. HE NOTIFIES MIDWAY.

BETWEEN 8:05 AND AND 8:28 A.M., THE SHIPS ARE ATTACKED BY SBDS, SB2U-3S, AND B-17S FROM MIDWAY.

NO HITS ARE SCORED BUT A SB2-U3 VINDICATOR, HIT BY ANTI-AIRCRAFT FIRE, CRASHES INTO MIKUMA.

THE RESULTING FIRE SPREADS TO THE ENGINE ROOM, SLOWING MIKUMA TO A CRAWL.

THE FOLLOWING DAY, JUNE 6, THREE MORE ATTACKS ARE MADE AGAINST THE CRUISERS BY SBDS FROM ENTERPRISE AND HORNET.

WOW! -- LOOK AT THAT BOAT BURN!

MIKUMA IS SO BADLY DAMAGED THAT IT IS ABANDONED AFTER THE THIRD ATTACK.

THE FIRES ARE SO HOT, NEARBY DESTROYER ARASHIO CAN'T GET CLOSE ENOUGH TO PULL OFF SURVIVORS.

MOGAMI IS LUCKY. IT IS HIT SIX TIMES BUT MANAGES TO ESCAPE.

MIKUMA FINALLY SINKS JUST AFTER SUNSET THAT DAY. 300 CREWMEN DIE.

MIKUMA IS THE LAST JAPANESE SHIP SUNK AT THE BATTLE OF MIDWAY. WITH IT GO ANY HOPES JAPAN HAS OF WINNING THE WAR.

THE END

THE ROAD TO RUIN

The loss at Midway spelled defeat in the war for Japan. Admiral Yamamoto realized that this failure against the Americans, just six months after the brilliant success at Pearl Harbor, had turned the tide against Japan. From now until the Japanese surrender in August 1945, Japan's war would be fought defensively against the furious attacks of America's ever-growing military might.

As America's power grew, Japan's shrivelled away. Without the natural resources or trained shipbuilders, Japan could not easily replace the ships it had lost. From the time of the attack on Pearl Harbor to June 1944, the United States built 117 aircraft carriers, the Japanese only 12. The American carriers were also of a superior quality and far better equipped than Japan's.

The loss of vital skills was also a crucial problem for the Japanese at Midway. The Imperial Navy's pilots and ground crews were shot down or killed on the ships destroyed at Midway. The Japanese did not have the time to replace them. New, inexperienced ground troops thrown into battle to stop the Americans had no time to be trained properly. Air crews had little flying practice, or combat training, due to

America dropped an atomic bomb on Hiroshima, Japan, on August 6, 1945. The devastation it caused led to Japan's official surrender on September 2 that year. (NARA)

▼

the fuel shortages and lack of time before the next battle.

But what if Japan had won the battle of Midway and destroyed the U.S. carriers? The entire course of the war could have been changed. The United States would have had to rebuild their aircraft carrier fleet, which could have hurt America's war efforts in supporting Europe against Germany. Also, by having to rebuild its navy, an American loss could also have slowed down the development of the atomic bomb that was going on in the United States by using up vital funds on building new ones.

The Japanese believed that the Americans were weak and had no will to fight. They thought their attack on Pearl Harbor had broken the spirit of the American people. But the attack actually united the American people and drove them to fight Japan. Americans wanted their attackers completely and totally defeated. They wanted revenge. By August 1945, that's exactly what they got. The road to the Japanese defeat began at the battle of Midway.

▲

Admiral Isoroku Yamamoto planned and commanded the attack on Midway, and knew that Japan's plan for control of the Pacific ended when their mighty carriers were lost in the battle. (NARA)

Mikuma was the last Japanese ship to be sunk at Midway. Much of the Japanese naval fleet was destroyed during the battle, and was never able to be replaced. (NARA)

▼

GLOSSARY

abandon — To leave and not intend to return.

aerial — Of, in, or caused by air or aircraft.

afloat — In a floating condition.

alert — To warn of approaching danger.

assault — A violent physical attack.

bearing — Direction, especially angular direction as used in navigation.

confirm — To establish the certainty of.

depth charge — An explosive charge designed for use underwater.

distract — To draw the attention away from something.

dogfight — A battle between fighter planes.

dusk — The time of evening just before darkness.

escort — One or more airplanes, warships, or other vehicles accompanying another or others to provide protection.

hunch — A suspicion or an intuition; a premonition.

inferno — A place or condition suggestive of hell, as in being chaotic, noisy, or intensely hot.

list — To tilt to one side.

magazine — In some firearms, a container in which cartridges are held until they pass into the chamber for firing.

maneuverable — The ability to make controlled changes in movement and direction.

port — The left side of a ship or aircraft, facing forward.

prime — First in degree or rank.

radar — The equipment used to detect distant objects and determine their characteristics by causing radio waves to be reflected from them and analyzing the results.

rudder — A flat movable piece of metal or wood in the stern of a vessel or the tail of an aircraft, used for directing the vehicle's course.

squadron — Any of various military units, as of soldiers, planes, or ships.

torpedo — A cylindrical, self-propelled underwater projectile launched from an airplane, a ship, or a submarine and designed to explode against or near a target.

ORGANIZATION

The International Midway Memorial Foundation
5530 Wisconsin Avenue
Suite 1147
Chevy Chase, MD 20815
001 (301) 652-0677
Web site: http://www.immf-midway.com/

Pilots of the Imperial Japanese Navy (left) and U.S. Army Air Force (right) spent much of the battle of Midway attacking each other's aircraft carriers. The destruction of the Japanese carrier fleet led ultimately to Japan's defeat in the war. (Chris Warner © Osprey Publishing Ltd.)

FOR FURTHER READING

Ballard, Robert D., and Rich Archbold. *Return to Midway*. Washington, D.C.: National Geographic Society, 1999.

Fuchida, Mitsuo, and Masatake Okumiya. *Midway: The Battle that Doomed Japan: The Japanese Navy's Story*. Annapolis, MD: The United States Naval Institute, 2001.

Healy, Mark. *Midway 1942: Turning Point in the Pacific*. Oxford, England: Osprey Publishing, 1994.

Worth, Richard. *Midway*. New York: Chelsea House Publications, 2002.

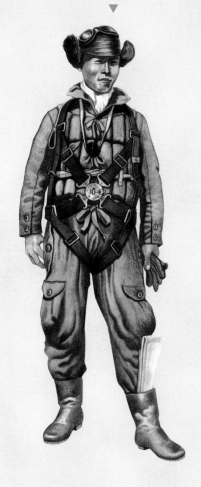

INDEX